THIS BOOK BELONGS TO...

Name:	Age:

Favourite player:

2022/2023

My Predictions...	Actual...

The Foxes' final position:

The Foxes' top scorer:

Premier League winners:

Premier League top scorer:

FA Cup winners:

EFL Cup winners:

Contributors: Peter Rogers, Andy Greeves

A TWOCAN PUBLICATION

©2022. Published by twocan under licence from Leicester City Football Club.

ISBN: 978-1-914588-76-1

£10

CONTENTS

CASTAGNE'S CRACKER

There were some great goals scored by the Foxes in 2021/22 as the club competed both domestically and in Europe too. However, for anyone among the 31,830 crowd inside King Power Stadium on Sunday 20 March, 2022 then Timothy Castagne's superb strike against Brentford will certainly live long in the memory.

The popular Belgian defender marked his return to Premier League action after an eight-match injury lay-off with a truly stunning strike to open the scoring in a 2-1 victory over the top-flight new boys.

There were 20 minutes on the clock when Harvey Barnes received possession in the left channel before cutting the ball back into the path of Castagne - the Belgian international who was outside the penalty area then took one touch before proceeding to hammer a swerving effort right into the top corner of the net.

The goal set the tone for the afternoon as James Maddison then added the Foxes' second goal of the game when he curled home a fantastic 25-yard free-kick just 13 minutes later.

For a player who is not really renowned for his goals, Castagne's rocket had a real element of surprise about it.

"No goalkeeper is saving that. That is an incredible strike and he will be delighted with that," acknowledged the co-commentator when taking a look at the replay of Castagne's incredible opener.

Castagne's face clearly showed his delight in marking his return to action in such a positive manner and the goal was enjoyed equally by his team-mates and of course the Foxes fans.

Having scored that memorable goal against the Bees in March 2022, Castagne was at it again against Thomas Frank's men just five months later when he headed home the club's first goal of the new 2022/23 Premier League season. Like all opening goals of a new campaign, the goal was met with great delight by the King Power faithful but just didn't quite have the wow factor of last season's missile!

NUMBER OF SEASONS
WITH THE FOXES:

6

LEICESTER CITY
LEAGUE APPEARANCES:

197

LEICESTER CITY LEAGUE GOALS:

46

LEGEND
EMILE HESKEY

FOXES ACHIEVEMENTS:

Football League Cup champions
winners 1996/97 & 1999/00

Football League First Division
Play-Offs 1996

PFA Young Player of the Year
runner-up 1997

MAJOR STRENGTH:

Creating
chances

INTERNATIONAL ACTION:

Heskey won 62 caps for England
and was an international player
for over a decade

FINEST HOUR:

Heskey scored the equalising
goal in Leicester's 1997 League
Cup final victory against
Middlesbrough

As strikers go, you couldn't get a more polar opposite pair than Emile Heskey and Jamie Vardy. If they had played at the same time, they would have made for a beautiful partnership!

While Heskey spent most of his time providing other players with goalscoring chances, Vardy is better known for finishing them off, as well as making blistering runs so that others could pick him out. Heskey was composed and intricate, and Vardy is lightning quick to sniff out a chance.

Both players assured their place in Leicester City folklore with their performances.

NUMBER OF SEASONS WITH THE FOXES:
10

LEICESTER CITY LEAGUE APPEARANCES:
386

LEICESTER CITY LEAGUE GOALS:
164

PLAYER OF THE SEASON WINNER:
2019/20
2015/16
(Premier League POS)

LEGEND

JAMIE VARDY

FOXES ACHIEVEMENTS:
Premier League champions 2015/16
FA Cup champions winners 2020/21
FA Community Shield winners 2021
Championship champions 2013/14

MAJOR STRENGTH:
Running in behind the defence
to chase a ball over the top
- and finishing with power

INTERNATIONAL ACTION:
Vardy scored a crucial goal in
England's 2-1 win over Wales
at EURO 2016, and was part of the
team who reached the FIFA World
Cup Semi-Finals in 2018

FINEST HOUR:
Scoring his 23rd goal of the
2019/20 season, securing
the Golden Boot. At 33,
he became the oldest ever
winner of the award

PATSON

DAKA

Defending is not just about stopping the attackers and clearing your lines. Making the best of possession you have just won is vital - although the danger has to be cleared, it is important for your team to keep hold of the ball.

SOCCER SKILLS
LONG PASSES

When passing your way out of defence, and short, side-foot passes are not possible, the longer pass, driven over the heads of midfield players, can be used.

EXERCISE

In an area 40m x 10m, A1 and A2 try to pass accurately to each other, with a defender B in the middle between them. Player B must attempt to stop the pass if possible, and A1 and A2 must keep the ball within the area of the grids.

After each successful long pass, the end player will exchange a shorter pass with B before passing long again, thus keeping the exercise realistic and also keeping the defender in the middle involved. The player in the middle should be changed every few minutes, and a 'count' of successful passes made for each player.

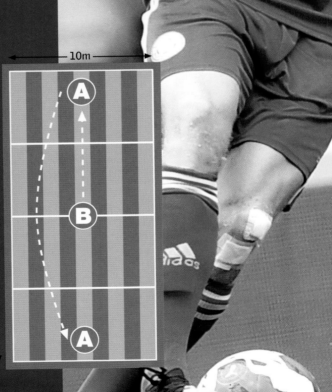

KEY FACTORS

1 Approach at an angle.
2 Non kicking foot placed next to the ball.
3 Eye on the ball.
4 Strike underneath the ball & follow through.

Practice is the key to striking a consistently accurate long pass and to developing the timing and power required.

The same end result could be achieved by bending the pass around the defender instead of over him, and this pass could be practised in the same exercise, by striking the football on its outer edge (instead of underneath) which will impart the spin required to make the ball 'bend' around the defender - not an easy skill!

2022/2023
PREMIER LEAGUE
SQUAD

1 DANNY WARD

GOALKEEPER DOB: 22/06/93 **COUNTRY:** WALES

A Wales international since 2016, Danny Ward joined Leicester City in 2018 as back-up to Kasper Schmeichel. When Foxes legend Schmeichel left for French side Nice this summer, Ward became Leicester's No.1 for the first time.

A smart shot-stopper with razor-like reactions, he progressed through the Wrexham academy, where he was born, before playing for Liverpool and Huddersfield Town.

2 JAMES JUSTIN
FULL-BACK DOB: 23/02/98 COUNTRY: ENGLAND

James Justin was signed by the Foxes in 2019 from Luton Town, where he had shone in previous seasons as the club moved up from League 2 to League 1.

A highly flexible full-back/wing-back who can play on either flank, Justin returned from a horrific injury during the 2021/22 season to regain his spot in the Leicester City first team and earn himself an England debut.

3 WOUT FAES
CENTRE-BACK DOB: 03/04/98 COUNTRY: BELGIUM

Wout Faes signed from French side Reims on transfer deadline day of summer 2022.

The centre-back from Belgium is a product of the prestigious Anderlecht academy in his homeland, and joined the Foxes for a reported fee of £15M. Faes made his debut for the Belgian national team in the UEFA Nations League in June 2022.

4 ÇAĞLAR SÖYÜNCÜ
CENTRE-BACK DOB: 23/05/96 COUNTRY: TURKEY

Çağlar Söyüncü is the perfect example of a modern-day centre-back. Physically robust yet comfortable with the ball between his feet, he represented the Foxes 28 times in the Premier League last season.

His best moment to date came in May 2021, when he netted the winner at Old Trafford as Leicester beat Manchester United away for the first time since 1998.

5 RYAN BERTRAND
LEFT-BACK DOB: 05/08/1989 COUNTRY: ENGLAND

Formerly of Chelsea and Southampton, Ryan Bertrand signed for the Foxes on a free transfer in the summer of 2021 and made his Foxes debut in the FA Community Shield soon after, in a famous win over Manchester City.

Capped 19 times by the England team at the time of writing, the 33-year-old left-back struggled for game-time in 2021/22, but will be looking for increased involvement in 2022/23.

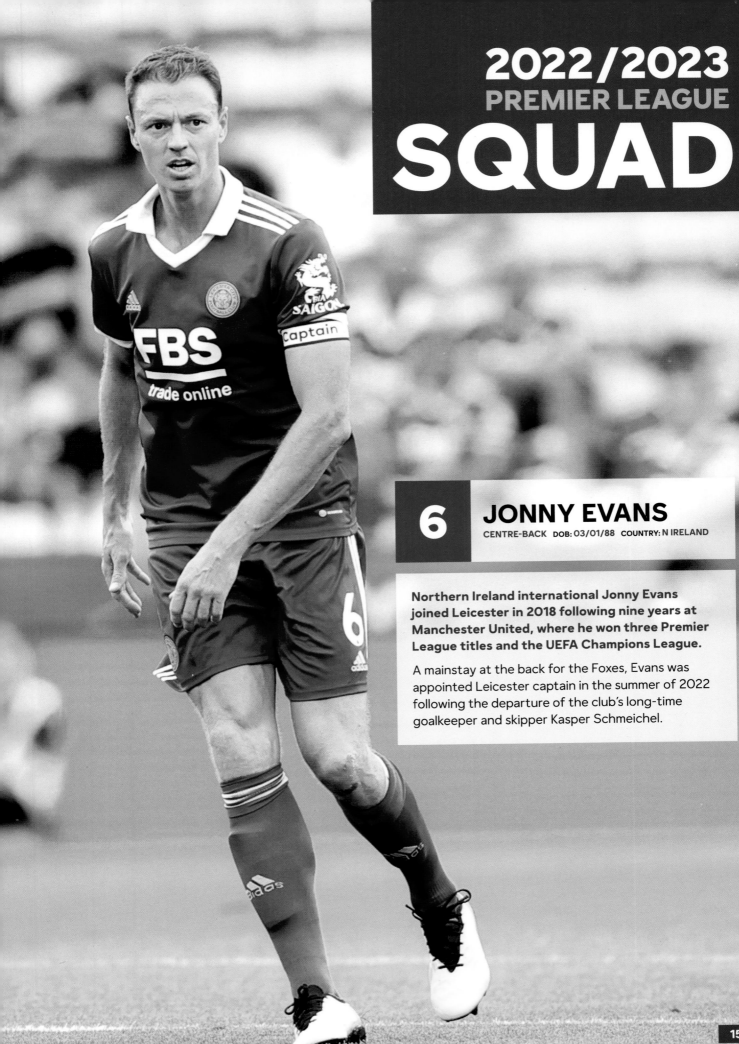

6   JONNY EVANS

CENTRE-BACK   DOB: 03/01/88   COUNTRY: N IRELAND

Northern Ireland international Jonny Evans joined Leicester in 2018 following nine years at Manchester United, where he won three Premier League titles and the UEFA Champions League.

A mainstay at the back for the Foxes, Evans was appointed Leicester captain in the summer of 2022 following the departure of the club's long-time goalkeeper and skipper Kasper Schmeichel.

7 HARVEY BARNES

LEFT-WINGER **DOB: 09/12/1997** **COUNTRY: ENGLAND**

Foxes favourite Harvey Barnes grew up in nearby Countesthorpe and joined the Club's Academy when he was just nine-years-old.

Exposure in the England youth set-ups - as well as loan spells with MK Dons, Barnsley and West Bromwich Albion - helped him hone his craft. Now the crafty winger is a Foxes star, a regular starter each week in the Premier League, and a senior England international.

8 YOURI TIELEMANS

CENTRAL MIDFIELDER **DOB: 07/05/97** **COUNTRY: BELGIUM**

Another Belgian in the current Leicester City squad, Youri Tielemans is a match-winner on his day. A master technician in midfield, he often pops up with crucial goals.

His most important strike to date came in the 2021 FA Cup Final, as the Foxes secured the trophy at the expense of soon-to-be European champions, Chelsea.

9 JAMIE VARDY

STRIKER   DOB: 11/01/87   COUNTRY: ENGLAND

A Leicester City legend and a Premier League great, Jamie Vardy is a rapid, technically capable and ruthless finisher with both feet.

A member of the Premier League 100 club and a goalscorer at EURO 2016 for England, Vardy has netted many memorable goals for Leicester City, including his outrageous dipping volley against Liverpool during the Foxes' title-winning season of 2015/16.

10 JAMES MADDISON

ATTACKING MIDFIELDER   DOB: 23/11/96   COUNTRY: ENGLAND

Ultra-popular among the King Power Stadium faithful, James Maddision is a free-kick extraordinaire, talented playmaker and a fiercely competitive leader.

Signed from Norwich City in 2018, he has gone on to establish himself as a Leicester City star with a keen eye for goal. In 2021/22, he notched 18 goals in all competitions for the Foxes from midfield.

11 **MARC ALBRIGHTON**
WINGER   DOB: 18/11/89   COUNTRY: ENGLAND

One of the heroes of Leicester City's miraculous Premier League-winning campaign of 2015/16, Marc Albrighton signed for the Foxes the season before, when the Foxes narrowly avoided relegation in their first season back in the top flight.

A willing runner even for a veteran of the club, young players look up to former Aston Villa man Albrighton for advice and inspiration.

12 **ALEX SMITHIES**
GOALKEEPER   DOB: 05/03/90   COUNTRY: ENGLAND

Alex Smithies was brought in this summer following three very strong seasons in the Championship as Cardiff City's No.1.

Yet to make his Leicester City debut, the 32-year-old will hope for chances in the first team in cup competitions this year. A Huddersfield Town legend, he moved to Queens Park Rangers in 2015, before joining Cardiff three years later.

14 KELECHI IHEANACHO
STRIKER DOB: 03/10/96 COUNTRY: NIGERIA

Kelechi Iheanacho burst onto the scene at Manchester City, during the 2015/16 and 2016/17 seasons, when he netted 21 times in 64 appearances.

His departure from the Etihad Stadium came as something of a surprise to many observers. One City's loss proved to be another City's gain. Leicester snapped up the Nigeria international in 2017, who bagged 47 goals in his first five seasons at the King Power Stadium, including 19 in all competitions in the 2020/21 season.

17 AYOZE PÉREZ
STRIKER DOB: 29/07/93 COUNTRY: SPAIN

Ayoze Pérez was born on the island of Tenerife, and after graduating through the Tenerife academy, quickly established himself as the club's star player.

After five successful years on Tyneside with Newcastle United, he became a Fox in 2019. Accurate off both feet and skilful in tight areas, the Spaniard was a member of the Leicester City side that won both the FA Cup and Community Shield in 2021.

18 DANIEL AMARTEY
RIGHT-BACK/CENTRE-BACK DOB: 21/12/1994
COUNTRY: GHANA

Daniel Amartey is a versatile player who can be deployed at centre-back, left-back, or even as a defensive midfielder.

An experienced Ghana international who hopes to represent his nation at the 2022 World Cup in Qatar, Amartey won the Premier League with Leicester in 2015/16, but it wasn't until last term when his involvement in the first team started to reach new levels.

20 PATSON DAKA
STRIKER DOB: 09/10/98 COUNTRY: ZAMBIA

It was Patson Daka's phenomenal strike rate of 54 league goals in 82 matches for Salzburg which alerted him to Leicester's scouts. Foxes fans have loved the Zambian ever since his move to the East Midlands in 2021.

His finest moment to date came in the 2021/22 UEFA Europa League campaign as he scored four goals in a 4–3 win over Spartak Moscow, becoming the first Leicester player to score four in one game since 1958 in the process.

21 RICARDO PEREIRA

RIGHT-BACK **DOB:** 06/10/93 **COUNTRY:** PORTUGAL

Injuries have plagued Ricardo Pereira's Leicester City career so far - which is a great shame given the level he can operate at when fully fit.

A 2018 signing from Portuguese giants Porto, Pereira's most memorable Foxes moment to date came last season, when his 88th-minute goal knocked PSV Eindhoven out of the UEFA Europa Conference League, and saw Leicester progress to the semi-final stage.

22 KIERNAN DEWSBURY-HALL

CENTRAL MIDFIELDER **DOB:** 06/09/98 **COUNTRY:** ENGLAND

Kiernan Dewsbury-Hall joined Leicester's academy in 2006, aged eight at the time. He was hardened for battle on loan at Luton Town during the 2020/21 before returning to King Power Stadium in 2021/22.

The all-action central midfielder packs a punch for a player of only 5ft 10in. He featured in the 2021/22 UEFA Europa Conference League Team of the Season for his part in the Foxes' march to the semi-finals that campaign.

23 JANNIK VESTERGAARD
CENTRE-BACK DOB: 03/08/92 COUNTRY: DENMARK

Part of the Denmark side which reached the semi-finals of the delayed UEFA EURO 2020 before falling to England, centre-back Jannik Vestergaard stands at a colossal 6ft 6in and has been a Foxes player since leaving Southampton in August 2021.

The Dane, who played 20 times for Leicester in 2021/22, is an obvious aerial threat from set-pieces given his height.

24 NAMPALYS MENDY
DEFENSIVE MIDFIELDER DOB: 23/06/92 COUNTRY: SENEGAL

French-born, Senegal international Nampalys Mendy has been a Fox since 2016, when he signed from Nice.

A cousin of former Swansea City striker Bafétimbi Gomis, Mendy won the FA Cup with Leicester City in 2021 and the Africa Cup of Nations the following year with his country. An aggressive holding midfielder, Mendy is a product of AS Monaco's academy.

25 WILFRED NDIDI

DEFENSIVE MIDFIELDER DOB: 16/12/96 COUNTRY: NIGERIA

A mainstay in Leicester's midfield ever since signing for the club for a reported £17M in the January window of 2017, Wilfred Ndidi has played more than 200 matches for the Foxes to date.

The Nigeria international is a master at turning over possession and allowing Leicester to transition from defence to attack. In 2019, he started studying for a degree in Business and Management at the city's De Montfort University.

26 DENNIS PRAET

CENTRAL MIDFIELDER DOB: 14/05/94 COUNTRY: BELGIUM

Dennis Praet spent the 2021/22 season on loan in Serie A at Torino but returned to King Power Stadium for the 2022/23 campaign.

Praet has been a Leicester City player since 2019 when he signed from Sampdoria for a reported £18M. He has gone on to establish himself as a valuable player for Brendan Rodgers' side. Praet has represented Belgium at every age group from under-15 to senior level.

27 TIMOTHY CASTAGNE
RIGHT-BACK DOB: 05/12/95 COUNTRY: BELGIUM

Just like James Justin, Belgian international Timothy Castagne is a versatile and flexible full-back who specialises as a wing-back and can play on either side and can even operate in a back three.

A lover of a deep cross arcing into the box for a striker to attack, he hugs the touchline and tries to get beyond his opposite number and to the byline.

31 DANIEL IVERSEN
GOALKEEPER DOB: 19/03/97 COUNTRY: DENMARK

Daniel Iversen spent the final two years of his youth career at Leicester City, having signed from Danish club Esbjerg. After a number of loan spells away from King Power Stadium, Iversen will compete with Ward and Smithies for the No.1 shirt this season.

He was the hero on his debut against Stockport County in the Carabao Cup in August 2022, saving three spot-kicks to help the Foxes through to the next round on penalties.

33 LUKE THOMAS
LEFT-BACK DOB: 10/06/2001 COUNTRY: ENGLAND

England U21 international Luke Thomas is a local lad from Syston who graduated through the Leicester City academy and now plays on the left flank for his boyhood club.

He made three Premier League appearances in the 2019/20 season and has steadily upped his involvement in the first team ever since. He made his European debut in the UEFA Europa League in August 2020 and also started for Leicester at Wembley Stadium in May 2021 as the Foxes lifted the Emirates FA Cup for the first time in the Club's history. At just 21 years old, he has a big career ahead of him.

42 BOUBAKARY SOUMARÉ
DEFENSIVE MIDFIELDER DOB: 27/02/99 COUNTRY: FRANCE

An experienced former France youth international, Boubakary Soumaré joined Leicester in the summer of 2021, arriving from Lille, where he had just played an integral part as they stunned Paris Saint-Germain to beat them to the Ligue 1 title.

Following 19 Premier League appearances for the Foxes in 2021/22, he'll look to continue to establish himself as a regular in the Foxes' starting XI this term.

MULTIPLE CHOICE

Here are 10 multiple choice questions to challenge your football knowledge!

Good luck...

ANSWERS ON PAGE 62

1. What was the name of Tottenham Hotspur's former ground?

A) White Rose Park
B) White Foot Way
C) White Hart Lane

2. Which club did Steven Gerrard leave to become Aston Villa manager?

A) Liverpool
B) Glasgow Rangers
C) LA Galaxy

3. Mohamed Salah and Son Heung-min were joint winners of the Premier League Golden Boot as the division's top scorers in 2021/22.

How many goals did they score?

A) 23   B) 24   C) 25

4. What is the nationality of Manchester United manager Erik ten Hag?

A) Swiss   B) Dutch
C) Swedish

5. Where do Everton play their home games?

A) Goodison Road
B) Goodison Way
C) Goodison Park

6. From which club did Arsenal sign goalkeeper Aaron Ramsdale?

A) Sheffield United
B) Stoke City
C) AFC Bournemouth

7. What is Raheem Sterling's middle name?

A) Shaun
B) Shaquille
C) Silver

8. Who won the 2021/22 League 1 Play-Off Final?

A) Wigan Athletic
B) Sunderland
C) Rotherham United

9. On how many occasions have Leicester City won the FA Cup?

A) Once
B) Twice
C) Three times

10. When Leicester City won the Premier League title in 2015/16, how many points did they end the campaign with?

A) 80 points
B) 81 points
C) 82 points

10
JAMES
MADDISON

ANSWERS ON PAGE 62

CLASSIC FAN-TASTIC

Filbert Fox is hiding in the crowd in five different places as Leicester City fans celebrate becoming Premier League champions in 2015/16. Can you find all five?

29

KIERNAN
DEWSBURY-HALL

22

Close control in tight situations creates havoc in opposition defences - particularly when receiving the ball in the air - and nine times out of 10, when a striker receives the ball, he has his back to goal.

SOCCER SKILLS
RECEIVING THE BALL

Quite often the ball will arrive in the air, and good strikers have to be able to cope with that - controlling and turning in one movement, ready for the instant shot.

EXERCISE 1

In an area 20m x 10m, two players A and A2 test the man in the middle, B, by initially throwing the ball at him in the air, with the instruction to turn and play in to the end man - if possible using only two touches.

The middle player is changed regularly, and to make things more realistic, the end players progress to chipping the ball into the middle.

The middle player is asked to receive and turn using chest, thigh, or instep.

KEY FACTORS

1 Assess flight early - get in position.
2 Cushion the ball.
3 Be half turned as you receive.

EXERCISE 2

A progression of this exercise is the following, where the ball is chipped or driven in to the striker from varying positions. He has to receive with his back to goal, and using just two touches in total if possible, shoot past the keeper into the goal!

To make this even more difficult, a defender can be brought in eventually. For younger children, the 'servers' should throw the ball to ensure consistent quality.

31

TRAIN TO WIN

Making sure that you are fit, healthy and fully prepared is key to success in whatever challenge you are taking on. Those three factors are certainly vital for professional footballers and also for any young aspiring player who plays for his or her school or local football team. The importance of fitness, health and preparation are key factors behind the work that goes into preparing the Leicester City players to perform at their maximum on matchday.

The Foxes players will need to demonstrate peak levels of fitness if they want to feature in Brendan Rodgers' team. Before anyone can think of pulling on a smart blue shirt and stepping out at King Power Stadium, they will have had to perform well at the LCFC Training Ground to have shown the manager, his coaches and fitness staff that they are fully fit and ready for the physical challenges that await them on a matchday.

Regardless of whether training takes place at the training ground or at the stadium, the players' fitness remains an all-important factor. Of course time spent practicing training drills and playing small-sided games will help a player's fitness but there is lots of work undertaken just to ensure maximum levels of fitness are reached.

Away from the training pitches the players will spend a great deal of time in the gymnasium partaking in their own personal work-outs. Bikes, treadmills and weights will all form part of helping the players reach and maintain a top level of fitness.

Over the course of a week the players will take part in many warm-up and aerobic sessions and even complete yoga and pilates classes to help with core strength and general fitness. The strength and conditioning coaches at the Club work tirelessly to do all they can to make sure that the players you see in action are at their physical peak come kick-off.

While the manager and his staff will select the team and agree the tactics, analysts will provide the players and staff with details on the opposition's strengths, weaknesses and their likely approach to the match.

Suffice to say the training ground is a busy place and no stone is left unturned in preparation for the big match!

PLAYER OF THE YEAR

JAMES MADDISON

Leicester City's End of Season Awards ceremony saw James Maddison crowned the Foxes' Player of the Season for 2021/22. The 25-year-old midfield star netted a phenomenal 18 goals as the Foxes competed on both domestic and European fronts in 2021/22 following their FA Cup success the previous season.

As the club's chief playmaker, Maddsion has consistently created openings and laid on chances for team-mates ever since he arrived at King Power Stadium from Norwich City in the summer or 2018. However, the fact that he continued to be the team's main creator while also weighing in with 18 goals made him the stand-out choice when supporters came to voting for their top performing Fox of 2021/22.

It was somewhat surprising that Maddison had to wait until the last week of October to grab his first goal of the season. After scoring what proved to be the winning goal in the Foxes' 2-1 win away to Brentford, Maddison never looked back on the goals front. He totalled 12 in the Premier League and also grabbed a brace in the 3-1 Europa Conference League victory away to Danish side Randers in February 2022.

Despite the team's disappointment at bowing out of the Europa Conference League at the semi-final stage in May, Maddison maintained his goalscoring standards when he was on target in each of the club's final four Premier League fixtures. His late flurry of goals include the final strike in our 3-0 victory over his former employers, Norwich City, plus an early goal against Chelsea at Stamford Bridge in a 1-1 draw in the penultimate game of the season.

Although Maddison was a regular goalscorer last season, the fact that he appears to get equal enjoyment from creating goals for others as he does from scoring them himself just goes to demonstrate his professionalism and commitment to the team.

The midfield maestro began the new 2022/23 Premier League season in similar vein as to how he ended the last campaign as he netted goals against both Arsenal and Southampton in the opening month of the season.

YOUNG PLAYER OF THE SEASON

The club's Young Player of the Season accolade was presented to Kiernan Dewsbury-Hall.

After returning to King Power Stadium following a successful and beneficial loan spell with Championship club Luton Town, the 24-year-old midfielder established himself as a passionate, creative and sensational talent in the Leicester City engine room as he made 44 appearances in all competitions.

Following such an impressive 2021/22 campaign, the popular midfielder agreed a new five-year contract with the Club ahead of the current season.

DREAM TEAM

Pick your ultimate Leicester City dream team and design them a kit!

YOURI
8
TIELEMANS

PREMIER LEAGUE
DANGER
MEN

20 TOP-FLIGHT STARS TO WATCH OUT FOR DURING 2022/23...

ARSENAL
GABRIEL JESUS

The Gunners completed the signing of Brazilian international striker Gabriel Jesus from Premier League champions Manchester City in July 2022.

A real penalty box predator, Jesus netted 95 goals in 236 appearances in a trophy-laden spell for City and Arsenal will be hopeful he can continue his impressive goals-to-games ratio at the Emirates Stadium.

ASTON VILLA
EMI BUENDÍA

Now in his second season at Villa Park, following a big money move from Norwich City, a great deal will be expected of Argentinean international midfielder Emi Buendia in 2022/23.

A highly skilful and creative player, Buendia has the ability to create chances for team-mates and score vital goals himself.

BOURNEMOUTH
KIEFFER MOORE

Giant front man Kieffer Moore chipped in with four goals in three games to help Bournemouth secure promotion to the Premier League last season.

The former Cardiff City man will be keen to prove his worth at Premier League level in 2022/23 in order to cement his place in Wales' squad for the 2022 FIFA World Cup finals in Qatar.

BRENTFORD
KEANE LEWIS-POTTER

England under-21 star Keane Lewis-Potter enjoyed an exceptional Championship campaign with Hull City in 2021/22 and that prompted Brentford to spend a club record fee to bring the exciting 21-year-old to West London.

A true attacker who can operate off of either flank, Lewis-Potter will be relishing the challenge of showcasing his skills at Premier League level.

BRIGHTON & HA
LEANDRO TROSSARD

After weighing in with eight Premier League goals last season, Belgian international winger Trossard has widely become recognised as the Seagulls' main creative force.

Hugging the left touchline and cutting inside to play in a team-mate or striking for goal himself, Trossard is another player who will be looking to feature in the forthcoming World Cup.

CRYSTAL PALACE
WILFRIED ZAHA

Players may come and go at Selhurst Park, but the constant threat offered by the Crystal Palace club legend Wilfried Zaha remains firmly in place.

An exciting forward who loves to take opponents on in one-on-one situations, Zaha has now amassed over 400 appearances for the club across his two spells at Selhurst Park, and will be looking to fly the Eagles into the top half of the Premier League table.

CHELSEA
MASON MOUNT

Having progressed through the academy system at Stamford Bridge, attacking midfielder Mason Mount has become one of the first names on both the Chelsea and England teamsheet.

Mount hit 11 Premier League goals last season and head coach Graham Potter will be keen to see more of the same as Chelsea look to put pressure on Liverpool and Manchester City in 2022/23.

EVERTON
JORDAN PICKFORD

Firmly established as first choice 'keeper for club and country, Jordan has been a reliable last line of defence for the Toffees since joining the club in summer 2017.

A host of match-saving saves last season were rewarded with the Player of the Season award and the England No.1 has now played over 200 games for Everton.

FULHAM
ALEKSANDAR MITROVIĆ

Having fired home a record-breaking 43 Championship goals for Fulham in their title-winning campaign last season, all eyes will be on Aleksandar Mitrović in 2022/23.

If Fulham are to shake off their yo-yo club tag, then the top-flight goalscoring form of their powerful Serbian striker is going to be key.

LIVERPOOL
MOHAMED SALAH

Together with goalkeeper Alisson and inspirational defender Virgil van Dijk, Liverpool forward Mo Salah has been the catalyst for the Reds' success in recent seasons.

The Egyptian superstar jointly topped the Premier League scoring charts with Spurs' Son Heung-min last season as Liverpool enjoyed a domestic cup double.

LEEDS UNITED
PATRICK BAMFORD

After suffering an injury-hit 2021/22, Leeds United striker Patrick Bamford will be hopeful that 2022/23 offers him the chance to demonstrate the form that won him a first full England cap in September 2021.

A versatile front man who can play as a lone striker or in a pair, Bamford can also operate as an attacking midfielder from either flank.

LEICESTER CITY
JAMIE VARDY

The goalscoring hero of Leicester City's sensational 2015/16 Premier League title triumph, striker Jamie Vardy once again topped the Foxes' scoring charts last season.

An energetic forward, full of running, Vardy never gives defenders a moment of peace, and will once again be the one to watch for goals at King Power Stadium in 2022/23.

MANCHESTER CITY
ERLING HAALAND

Manchester City pulled off the biggest summer transfer coup when they lured Norwegian striker Erling Haaland from Borussia Dortmund to the Etihad Stadium for 2022/23.

Boasting a phenomenal strike rate at Dortmund and with his national team too, Haaland is sure to bring goals galore to the Premier League champions.

MANCHESTER UNITED
BRUNO FERNANDES

Attacking midfielder Bruno has become the heartbeat of the Red Devils' forward play since signing from Sporting Lisbon.

Blessed with a wide range of passing skills, the 28-year-old Portuguese international has the knack of unlocking even the tightest of defences.

TOTTENHAM HOTSPUR
SON HEUNG-MIN

South Korean superstar Son ended the 2021/22 season by picking up the Premier League Golden Boot as joint top goalscorer along with Liverpool's Mohamed Salah.

Forming an almost telepathic partnership with England captain Harry Kane, Tottenham Hotspur will certainly be a team to watch if Son repeats his lethal form in front of goal again in 2022/23.

NEWCASTLE UNITED
BRUNO GUIMARÃES

After joining the Magpies from Lyon in January 2022, Brazilian midfielder Bruno has become a real cult hero with the fans at St. James' Park.

Bruno scored five Premier League goals in 17 games last season and looks set to be one of the first names on Eddie Howe's teamsheet in 22/23.

WEST HAM UNITED
JARROD BOWEN

Blessed with the ability to operate in a variety of attacking positions, Jarrod Bowen enjoyed an exceptional 2021/22 campaign.

The 25-year-old netted 18 goals in all competitions and made 51 appearances as the Hammers enjoyed a top-half finish and reached the semi-finals of the Europa League. He was also handed an England debut in June 2022.

NOTTINGHAM FOREST
DEAN HENDERSON

Forest made a real statement of intent following their promotion to the Premier League when they completed the season-long loan signing of the Man Utd keeper.

Capped by England, Henderson will hope his City Ground performances can push him into England manager Gareth Southgate's thoughts for the 2022 FIFA World Cup finals in Qatar.

WOLVES
GONÇALO GUEDES

Wanderers boosted their attacking options when they completed the signing of Portugal forward Gonçalo Guedes from Valencia at the start of the 2022/23 season.

Capped on over 30 occasions by Portugal, the 25-year-old is well known to Wolves' manager Bruno Lage having played for him at Benfica earlier in his career.

SOUTHAMPTON
JAMES WARD-PROWSE

One of the very best dead ball deliverers, Saints skipper Ward-Prowse has progressed through the academy ranks at St. Mary's to play over 350 first-team games for the club.

James is another England star who will hope to be on the plane for Qatar 2022.

41

11

MARC ALBRIGHTON

Here are ten fun football true or false teasers for you to tackle!

TRUE OR FALSE?

ANSWERS ON PAGE 62

1. England star Harry Kane has only ever played club football for Spurs

2. The FIFA World Cup in 2026 is due to be hosted in the USA, Mexico and Canada

3. Manchester City's former ground was called Maine Park

4. Liverpool's Jürgen Klopp has never managed the German national team

5. Gareth Southgate succeeded Roy Hodgson as England manager

6. Manchester United's Old Trafford has the largest capacity in the Premier League

7. Jordan Pickford began his career at Everton

8. Huddersfield Town's nickname is the Terriers

9. The Foxes signed James Maddison from Coventry City

10. In the 2021/22 season, Jamie Vardy topped the Foxes' Premier League scoring charts with 15 goals

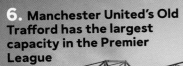

43

NUMBER OF SEASONS WITH THE FOXES:

9

LEICESTER CITY LEAGUE APPEARANCES:

323

LEICESTER CITY LEAGUE GOALS:

14

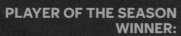

PLAYER OF THE SEASON WINNER:

2012/13

LEGEND

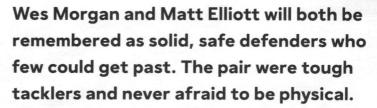

WES MORGAN

LEICESTER CITY ACHIEVEMENTS:

Premier League champions 2015/16

FA Cup champions winners 2020/21

Football League Championship champions 2013/14

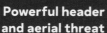

MAJOR STRENGTH:

Powerful header and aerial threat

INTERNATIONAL ACTION:

Morgan earned 30 caps for Jamaica between 2013 and 2016

FINEST HOUR:

Morgan played a memorable part in Leicester's 2-0 win over Sevilla to reach the UEFA Champions League Quarter-Finals by scoring the first goal of the game

Wes Morgan and Matt Elliott will both be remembered as solid, safe defenders who few could get past. The pair were tough tacklers and never afraid to be physical.

Morgan and Elliott enjoyed long spells with the Club, during fruitful eras for the Foxes. Not by coincidence, they each played a big role in the success of their respective teams.

Here are some facts about each of them...

LEGEND

MATT ELLIOTT

NUMBER OF SEASONS WITH THE FOXES:

8

LEICESTER CITY LEAGUE APPEARANCES:

279

LEICESTER CITY LEAGUE GOALS:

32

LEICESTER CITY ACHIEVEMENTS:

League Cup champions winners 1998/99

First Division runners-up 2002/03

MAJOR STRENGTH:

Tough tackling and brute strength

INTERNATIONAL ACTION:

Eligible, through his grandmother, to play for Scotland, he won all of his international appearances while at Leicester

FINEST HOUR:

Scoring both goals in the League Cup Final to beat Tranmere 2-1 in 1999

CLUB SEARCH

```
M A S D D E T I N U R E T S E H C N A M
K P W H M F Y A G I S G F Z E N O P H S
S M A N C H E S T E R C I T Y J B F O E
W N A E L T G I R C I A S B D R I U J T
K E F R U P S T O H M A H N E T T O T G
H Q S B D D B L B S V U S N D H O R S B
C A F T X E H O R Y S N T H A K J M E E
A G Y J H W T U O Q C F N M C A L V R C
U O U T S A R I L P O D P K L P E A O A
H T S U I G M A N R A T P L U R T D F L
T P T H P C N U D U O M I S T A F E M A
U I T W V E R A N N E V F O W E P G A P
O R M E S J W E P I N L N L E S U L H L
M O K R O S U V T O T A T M N L C I G A
E M A H L U F G T S K E K S D E B M N T
N N L D Q F C S N P E W D H A H O A I S
R S I A J B A O A S Y C B O O C N X T Y
U H D R Z L O O P R E V I L U L W J T R
O T E C D E T I N U S D E E L R A E O C
B R I G H T O N & H O V E A L B I O N T
```

Arsenal
Aston Villa
Bournemouth
Brentford
Brighton & Hove Albion

Chelsea
Crystal Palace
Everton
Fulham
Leeds United
Leicester City

Liverpool
Manchester City
Manchester United
Newcastle United
Nottingham Forest

Southampton
Tottenham Hotspur
West Ham United
Wolverhampton Wanderers

ANSWERS ON PAGE 62

WILFRED

NDIDI

25

WHICH BALL?

Can you work out which is the actual match ball in these two action pics?

ANSWERS ON PAGE 62

NAME THE SEASON

Can you recall the campaign when these magic moments occured?

1. In which season did Chelsea last win the UEFA Champions League?

2. When were Manchester United last Premier League champions?

3. At the end of which season were England crowned World Cup winners?

4. In which season did Aleksandar Mitrović net 43 Championship goals for Fulham?

5. In which season did Leicester City become Premier League champions?

6. When did Tottenham Hotspur last reach the League Cup Final?

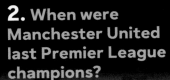

7. In which season were Sheffield United last promoted to the Premier League?

8. When did Manchester City win their first Premier League title?

9. During which season did Leicester City last win the League Cup?

10. In which season did James Maddison win his first senior cap for England?

49

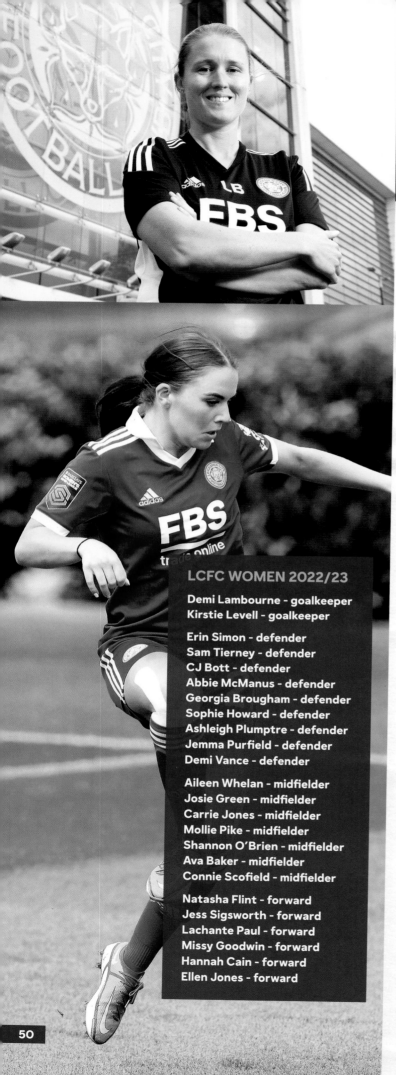

LCFC WOMEN

After England's fantastic achievement in winning the UEFA Women's European Championships in the summer of 2022, the profile of girls and women's football continues to grow and grow.

However, it wasn't just the Lionesses who enjoyed a historic 2021/22 campaign. Having won the Barclays Women's Championship title in 2020/21 and securing a place in the Barclays Women's Super League, the 2021/22 season was a historic campaign for LCFC Women.

Competing for the first time against the very best that the women's game has to offer, the Foxes' really rose to the challenge of the Barclays Women's Super League following the appointment of new manager Lydia Bedford.

A UEFA Pro Licence coach, Bedford was appointed manager in November 2021 and swiftly set about making the team a competitive force in the Barclays Women's Super League. As a newly promoted Club, the Foxes' eventually managed to maintain their top-flight status when they finished 11th in the table. Having survived relegation at the expense of the Birmingham City Women who propped up the league table in 12th, Bedford agreed a new two-year deal as the Club aims to establish itself among the elite of the women's game.

As well as running the high-profile first team at WSL level, Leicester City are fully committed to the women's game at all levels and have an Academy setup which caters for girls at all age groups from under-9s to under-21s, training and playing home games at the Belvoir Drive training complex.

Full details of the LCFC Women's team and their 2022/23 fixtures can be found on the Club's official website: www.lcfc.com/women

LCFC WOMEN 2022/23

Demi Lambourne - goalkeeper
Kirstie Levell - goalkeeper

Erin Simon - defender
Sam Tierney - defender
CJ Bott - defender
Abbie McManus - defender
Georgia Brougham - defender
Sophie Howard - defender
Ashleigh Plumptre - defender
Jemma Purfield - defender
Demi Vance - defender

Aileen Whelan - midfielder
Josie Green - midfielder
Carrie Jones - midfielder
Mollie Pike - midfielder
Shannon O'Brien - midfielder
Ava Baker - midfielder
Connie Scofield - midfielder

Natasha Flint - forward
Jess Sigsworth - forward
Lachante Paul - forward
Missy Goodwin - forward
Hannah Cain - forward
Ellen Jones - forward

1. WHO AM I?

2. WHO AM I?

3. WHO AM I?

4. WHO AM I?

52

Can you figure out who each of these Foxes stars are?

WHO ARE YOU?

5. WHO AM I?

6. WHO AM I?

7. WHO AM I?

8. WHO AM I?

ANSWERS ON PAGE 62

53

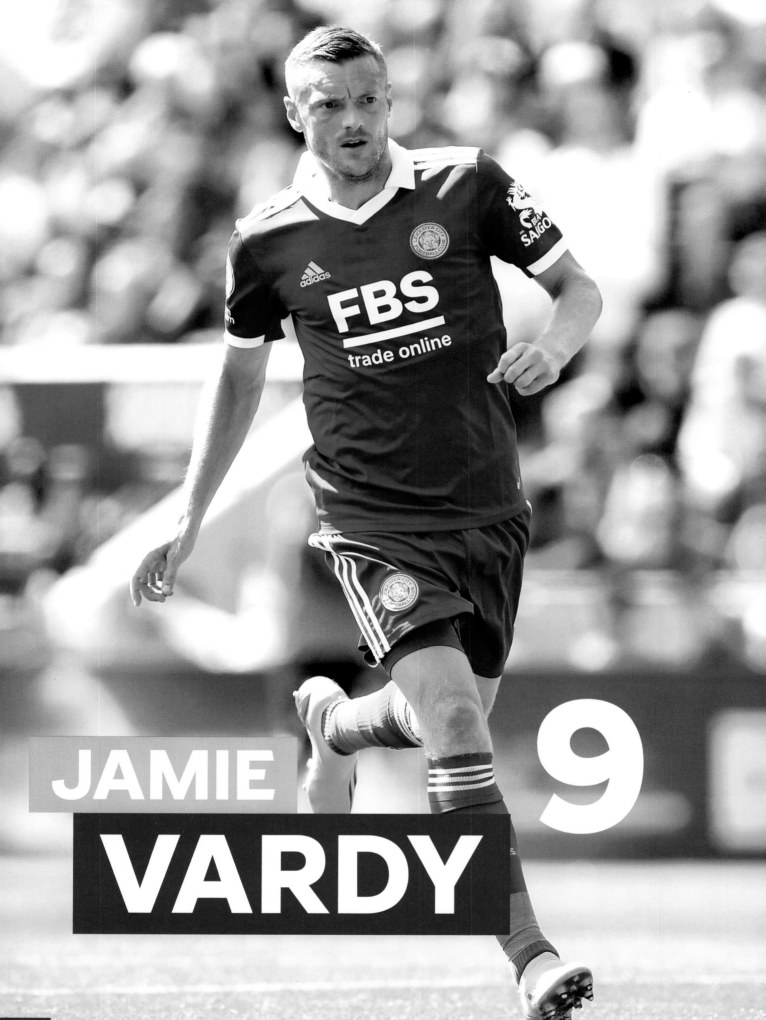

JAMIE
VARDY

9

Can you colour
in this picture
of Jamie Vardy?

TRUE

COLOURS

55

PREMIER LEAGUE CHAMPIONS
Liverpool

FAST >> FORWARD

Do your predictions for 2022/23 match our own?...

CHAMPIONSHIP WINNERS
Millwall

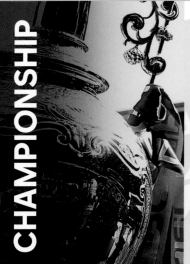

CHAMPIONSHIP RUNNERS-UP
Norwich City

PREMIER LEAGUE RUNNERS-UP
Chelsea

PREMIER LEAGUE

PREMIER LEAGUE TOP SCORER
Jamie Vardy

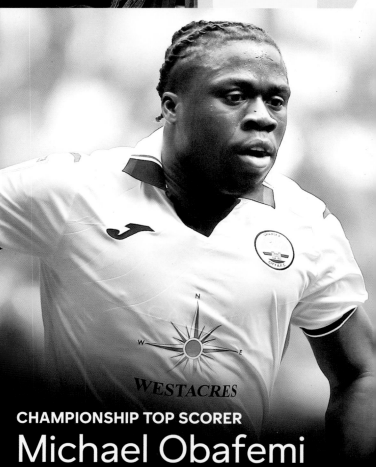

CHAMPIONSHIP TOP SCORER
Michael Obafemi

56

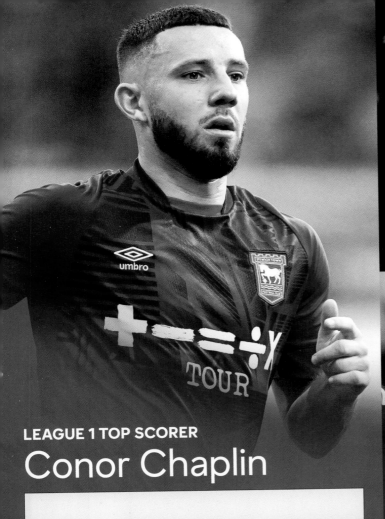

LEAGUE 1 TOP SCORER
Conor Chaplin

FA CUP WINNERS
Spurs

LEAGUE CUP WINNERS
Leicester City

LEAGUE 1 CHAMPIONS
Ipswich Town

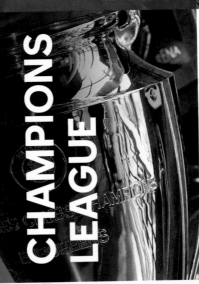

CHAMPIONS LEAGUE WINNERS
Real Madrid

LEAGUE 1 RUNNERS-UP
Oxford United

EUROPA LEAGUE WINNERS
Roma

57

NUMBER OF SEASONS
WITH THE FOXES:

7

LEICESTER CITY
LEAGUE APPEARANCES:

216

LEICESTER CITY
LEAGUE GOALS:

103

LEGEND

GARY LINEKER

LEICESTER CITY
ACHIEVEMENTS:

**Football League Second Division
champions 1979/80**

MAJOR STRENGTH:

**Always being in the right place
at the right time to score**

INTERNATIONAL ACTION:

**Lineker remains one of England's
greatest-ever strikers with
48 international goals to his
name in just 80 caps - and
a World Cup Golden Boot**

FINEST HOUR:

**Making his debut for his boyhood
club on New Year's Day in a 2-0
win over Oldham Athletic**

Two of the best strikers Leicester City
have had throughout their illustrious
history are Gary Lineker and Alan Smith.

Lineker and Smith were classic poachers.
Ironically, they could both be described as 'fox in
the box' strikers for the Foxes. The pair are mostly
remembered for always being in the right place
at the right time to knock the ball home.

This was enough to earn both of them a lot
of respect and a lot of appearances for the
Club.

NUMBER OF SEASONS WITH THE FOXES:

5

LEICESTER CITY LEAGUE APPEARANCES:

217

LEICESTER CITY LEAGUE GOALS:

84

LEGEND

ALAN SMITH

LEICESTER CITY ACHIEVEMENTS:

Promotion to First Division 1982/83

MAJOR STRENGTH:

Dangerous in the air with superb heading ability

INTERNATIONAL ACTION:

Smith played 13 times for England, scoring two goals

FINEST HOUR:

Scoring his 13th goal of the 1982/83 season, helping Leicester gain promotion to the First Division

IDENTIFY THE STAR

Can you put a name to the football stars in these 10 teasers?

Good luck...

ANSWERS ON PAGE 62

1. Manchester City's title-winning 'keeper Ederson shared the 2021/22 Golden Glove award for the number of clean sheets with which Premier League rival?

2. Which Portuguese superstar re-joined Manchester United in the 2021/22 season?

3. Can you name the Brazilian midfielder who joined Aston Villa in May 2022 following a loan spell at Villa Park?

4. Who became Arsenal manager in 2019?

5. Who scored the winning goal in the 2021/22 UEFA Champions League Final?

6. After 550 games for West Ham United, which long-serving midfielder announced his retirement in 2022?

7. Who took the mantle of scoring Brentford's first Premier League goal?

8. Who scored the final goal for Manchester City in their 2021/22 Premier League title-winning season?

9. Who scored Leicester City's final goal of the 2015/16 Premier League title-winning season?

10. Can you name the former Spain U21 international who joined the Foxes in the summer of 2019?

60

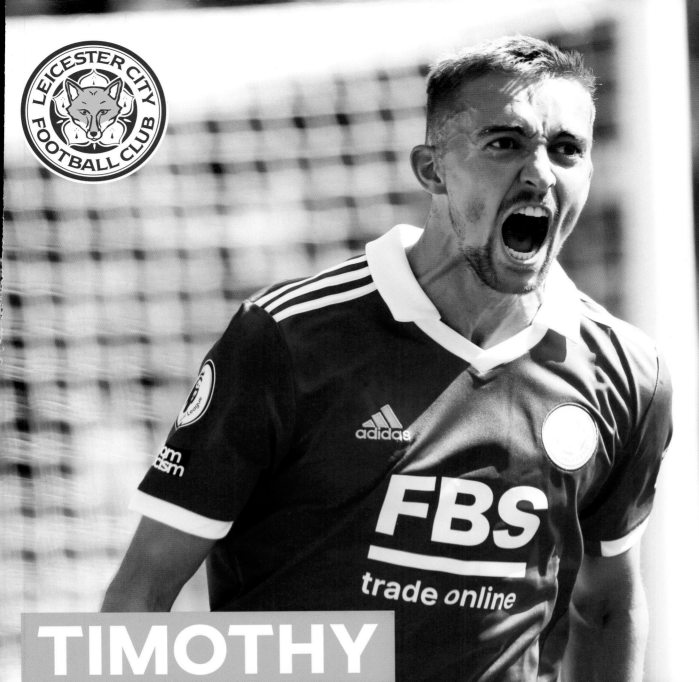

TIMOTHY

CASTAGNE

27

ANSWERS

PAGE 26 · MULTIPLE CHOICE

1. C. 2. B. 3. A. 4. B. 5. C. 6. A. 7. B. 8. B. 9. A. 10. B.

PAGE 28 · FAN'TASTIC

PAGE 43 · TRUE OR FALSE?

1. False, Harry played on loan for Leyton Orient, Millwall, Norwich City & Leicester City. 2. True. 3. False, it was called Maine Road. 4. True. 5. False, Gareth succeeded Sam Allardyce. 6. True. 7. False, Jordan began his career at Sunderland. 8. True. 9. False, he was signed from Norwich City. 10. True.

PAGE 46 · CLUB SEARCH

Wolverhampton Wanderers

PAGE 48 · WHICH BALL?

PAGE 49 · NAME THE SEASON

1. 2020/21. 2. 2012/13. 3. 1965/66. 4. 2021/22. 5. 2015/16. 6. 2020/21. 7. 2018/19. 8. 2011/12. 9. 1999/2000. 10. 2019/20.

PAGE 52 · WHO ARE YOU?

1. Kelechi Iheanacho. 2. James Justin. 3. Timothy Castagne. 4. Çağlar Söyüncü. 5. Jamie Vardy. 6. Harvey Barnes. 7. Jonny Evans. 8. James Maddison.

PAGE 60 · IDENTIFY THE STAR

1. Allison Becker. 2. Cristiano Ronaldo. 3. Philippe Coutinho. 4. Mikel Arteta. 5. Vinicius Junior. 6. Mark Noble. 7. Sergi Canos. 8. Ilkay Gundogan. 9. Danny Drinkwater. 10. Ayoze Pérez.